DOGS AND PUPPIES

Collector Card

DOGS AND PUPPIES

Collector Card

DOGS AND PUPPIES

Collector Card

DOGS AND PUPPIES

Collector Card

Saluki

Fast and elegant hound that hunted gazelles with the Ancient Egyptians.

	SCORE
FIRST KNOWN: 3000 BCE	10
BEAUTY: elegant	6
MAX HEIGHT: 27.5 in. (70cm)	9
HAIR LENGTH: long	7

Komondor

A dog in sheep's clothing: this dreadlocked dog guards sheep.

	SCORE
FIRST KNOWN: 800s CE	8
BEAUTY: exotic	5
MAX HEIGHT: 31 in. (80cm)	10
HAIR LENGTH: very long	10

Poodle

Energetic and intelligent, this dog is recognized by its curly coat.

	SCORE
FIRST KNOWN: 1500s	4
BEAUTY: curly fur	10
MAX HEIGHT: 24 in. (60cm)	8
HAIR LENGTH: medium	6

Pug

This popular little dog has a famous face and a little curled tail.

	SCORE
FIRST KNOWN: 300s CE	5
BEAUTY: very cute	8
MAX HEIGHT: 12 in. (30cm)	4
HAIR LENGTH: short	4

It's all about . . .

DOGS AND PUPPIES

KINGFISHER

LONDON & NEW YORK

Distributed in the U.S. and Canada by Macmillan,
175 Fifth Ave., New York, NY 10010

Library of Congress Cataloging-in-Publication data
has been applied for.

Series editor: Sarah Snashall
Series design: Anthony Hannant (Little Red Ant)
Written by Sarah Snashall

ISBN: 978-0-7534-7410-5

Kingfisher books are available for special promotions
and premiums. For details contact: Special Markets
Department, Macmillan, 175 Fifth Ave.,
New York, NY 10010.

For more information, please visit
www.kingfisherbooks.com

Printed in China
9 8 7 6 5 4 3 2 1
1TR/1117/WKT/UG/105MA

Picture credits
The Publisher would like to thank the following for permission to reproduce their material.
Top = t; Bottom = b; Center = c; Left = l; Right = r
Cover iStock/Phonlamal Photo, back cover iStock/Sensor spot; pages 2–3, 30–31 iStock/
dageldog; 4 iStock/animalinfo; 4–5b iStock/MirasWonderland; 5t iStock/alexei_tm;
6b iStock/TeoLazarev; 6r iStock/Diyanski; 7t iStock/Eriklam; 7cl iStock/anna-av;
7b Shutterstock/Melounix; 8 iStock/Himagine; 9t Shutterstock/Natalia V Guseva; 9c Getty/
Auscape; 10–11 iStock/GlobalP; 11b iStock/igorr1; 12 iStock/LexitheMonster; 13t iStock/
EcoPic; 13b iStock/alvarez; 14 iStock/ventdusud; 15t iStock/cyclonphoto; 15b Alamy/Edwin
Remsburg; 16 Alamy/615 collection; 17t Alamy/tony french; 17b Alamy/SPUTNIK; 18 Alamy/
Classic Image; 19 iStock/fotofrankyat; 19br iStock/rohappy; 20 iStock/suriyasilsaksom;
21t iStock/crisserbug; 21c Alamy/JuniorsBildarchive GmbH; 21b Alamy/DK; 22 iStock/
wundervisuals; 23t Rex/Shutterstock/Virginamerica; 23c Shutterstock/otsphoto;
23b iStock/artpipi; 24 iStock/mato181; 25t iStock/Astakhova; 25b iStock/KateDobies;
26 iStock/kali9; 27t iStock/s5iztok; 27b iStock/Chuckee; 28 iStock/f8grapher;
29t iStock/lurlisokolov; 29b iStock/Sladic.
Cards: front tl Shutterstock/Manfred Ruckszio; tr Shutterstock/Everita Pane; bl iStock/
Ivanastar; br iStock/nimis69; back tl iStock/Alphotographic; tr Alamy/Farlap; bl iStock/
Bessudov_Sergey; br iStock/shanecotee.

Front cover: An excited terrier puppy runs through grass.

CONTENTS

We love dogs!

Dogs have been living with humans for at least 10,000 years. For thousands of years, dogs helped people hunt for food. Today most dogs are pets, though many work as sheep dogs, police dogs, and guide dogs.

Dogs come in many different shapes, sizes, and color patterns.

Dogs are loyal and intelligent animals;
they are playful and affectionate.

Big and small

All domestic dogs belong to one species of dog. But over thousands of years hundreds of very different-looking breeds of dog have developed.

We organize dog breeds into six groups:
Companion dogs
Working dogs
Terriers
Hounds
Sporting dogs
Herding dogs

The fast Borzoi was bred to hunt wolves.

English setters have a long, speckled coat.

The Great Dane is massive compared to the tiny Chihuahua.

Corgis are a favorite breed of Britain's Queen Elizabeth II.

Bull terriers have an egg-shaped face and triangular-shaped eyes.

All shapes and sizes

The biggest dog is the Great Dane; the smallest dog is the Chihuahua. The Komondor has the strangest hair; the Xoloitzcuintli (say *showlo-its-kwint-lee*) has no hair at all on its body.

Fastest dog: Greyhound
Longest hair: Komondor and Afghan Hound
Largest dog: Great Dane
Smallest dog: Chihuahua
Smartest dog: Border Collie

A greyhound is the fastest dog. It can run at 43 miles (70 kilometers) an hour.

The Bedlington terrier's curly coat makes it look like a lamb.

The Xoloitzcuintli only has hair on its head.

The Border Collie is one of the most intelligent dogs.

Strong and lean

The domestic dog is a cousin of the gray wolf. With its strong legs and lean body, the dog is still a hunting animal.

FACT ...

A dog licks its nose to pick up scent particles that land on it.

tail—for communication

claws

footpads—protect feet and make it easier to run

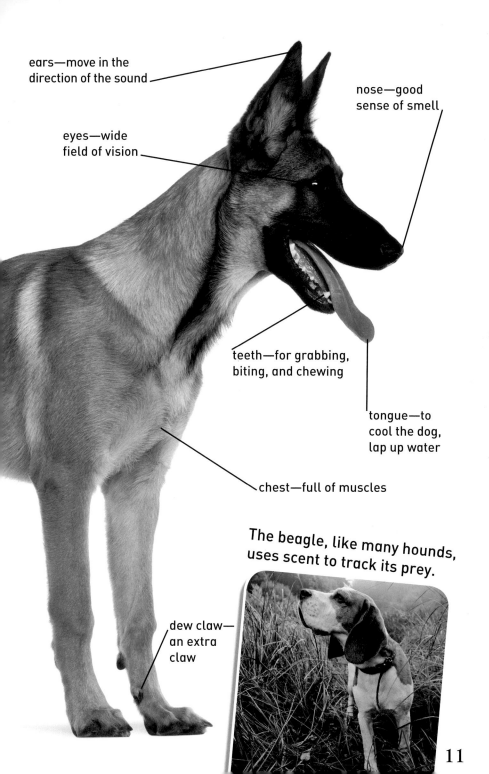

ears—move in the
direction of the sound

nose—good
sense of smell

eyes—wide
field of vision

teeth—for grabbing,
biting, and chewing

tongue—to
cool the dog,
lap up water

chest—full of muscles

dew claw—
an extra
claw

The beagle, like many hounds,
uses scent to track its prey.

11

Hunters and chasers

Sporting dogs, hounds, and terriers are bred for tracking and hunting animals. They have stamina and speed and strong hunting instincts. As pets, they need lots of exercise.

When a pointer detects prey, it freezes and "points" with its nose.

SPOTLIGHT: Mick the Miller

Famous for: first sporting superstar who won 51 of his 68 races
Breed: greyhound
Owned by: Father Martin Brophy, Ireland

Once hunting dogs in Ancient Egypt, greyhounds are now famous as racing dogs.

FACT ...

Dalmatians were trained to run alongside stagecoaches to protect them from highwaymen.

13

Herders and workers

Dogs are intelligent and can be trained to work for us. Herding dogs guard and herd sheep and cattle. Working dogs guard houses and pull sleds. Service dogs help people who have limited sight or hearing, or difficulty in getting around.

Sled dog teams follow commands to turn left or right.

FACT ...

In 1925, twenty sled dog teams traveled 674 miles (1085 kilometers) in relay in five and a half days. They traveled from Nenana to Nome in Alaska, USA, to deliver life-saving medicine.

Guide dogs are trained when they are puppies to help people with little or no eyesight move around safely.

Smart Border Collies herd a flock of sheep into a pen, or move them from field to field.

A dangerous job

Labrador retrievers and German shepherd dogs are strong and quick to learn. Well-trained dogs support the police, search for people after a disaster, or work as guard dogs. Military dogs can find explosives and track enemies.

Military dogs sometimes wear special goggles to protect their eyes.

This search and rescue dog is trained to jump out of a helicopter to rescue people who are drowning.

SPOTLIGHT: Veterok and Ugolyok

Famous for: the longest spaceflight made by dogs—22 days!

Breed: mixed

Owned by: Russian Space Programme

Surviving the cold

Some working dogs have a thick double layer of fur. They work in cold places in the far north of the world, pulling sleds, hunting elk, saving lives, and exploring.

Norwegian explorer Roald Amundsen took teams of Greenland dogs on his 1911 expedition to the South Pole.

Famous for:	rescuing 40 people who became lost in the Alps
Breed:	St. Bernard
Owner:	monks in Switzerland

FACT...

St. Bernard rescue dogs were trained to lick the people they found until they were warm.

Samoyeds have a thick double coat so they can survive very low temperatures.

19

Puppies!

A mother dog will have a litter of about five or six puppies at the same time. When the puppies are born, they are helpless—they cannot see or hear. They spend most of their first days asleep.

The mother dog will nurse her puppies for about six weeks.

The blind and deaf puppies snuggle up to their littermates for comfort.

The mother licks her new puppies clean.

FACT ...

Most Dalmatian puppies are born all white with no spots.

At three weeks puppies begin to stand up.

Growing up

Puppies usually stay with their mother for about eight to ten weeks. By this time they can walk and eat solid food. They are ready to find a new home.

Owners need to give their puppies plenty of attention and affection.

Famous for: having millions of internet fans and his own cuddly toy on sale

Breed: Pomeranian

Owned by: Irene Ahn, San Francisco

Puppies play fight with their brothers and sisters.

Puppies have lots of energy.

23

Understanding your puppy

It is important to understand your puppy. Your puppy raises or lowers its ears if it is happy or sad. It might growl or thump its tail when angry.

If your puppy lowers its front legs and wags its tail, it wants to play.

When a dog is scared it will put its tail between its legs, flatten its ears, and drop its head.

FACT ...

Dogs circle around before going to sleep. In the wild, this was done to flatten the grass to make a more comfortable sleeping place.

Dogs sniff each other to find out about one another.

Training

We train puppies to follow our commands by using rewards and giving praise. This helps to keep them safe both at home and outside.

You can teach your puppy to follow commands such as Sit, Stay, Come, and Lie down.

Dogs can show off their training on an agility course at a dog show.

Intelligent dogs can be trained to do tricks—and even surf!

Caring for your dog

Your dog needs lots of affection, attention, and a place to sleep; it needs the right food and exercise. It also needs you to check its teeth and general health, and make sure it gets the right vaccinations from a vet.

You should groom your dog regularly to keep its fur clean.

Dogs need to have exercise every day. Working dogs and sporting breeds, such as this retriever, need long walks.

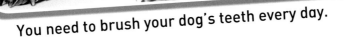
You need to brush your dog's teeth every day.

GLOSSARY

agility course A series of obstacles for a dog to go through successfully as fast as possible.

breed A group of animals that all look very similar.

communication Telling others what you are thinking or feeling.

domestic Tamed to live safely with humans.

explosive Chemicals that can blow things up.

herding Gathering together a group of animals, such as sheep.

highwayman A person who used to attack stagecoaches to steal money and valuables from travelers.

instinct Knowing without being taught.

intelligent Smart.

lean Thin and strong.